*Rediscovering the Rosary*

Gabriel Harty O.P.

# *Rediscovering the Rosary*

Veritas Publications Dublin

First published 1979 by
Veritas Publications,
7-8 Lower Abbey Street,
Dublin 1.



Cover design by Richard Whyte

Cover photographs by Donal J. Barry

Imprimi potest:
Damian Byrne, O.P.,
Prior Provincial,
July 1979

Nihil Obstat:
Richard Sherry, D.D.,
Censor Deputatus

Imprimatur:
+ Dermot,
Archbishop of Dublin,
July 1979

The *nihil obstat* and *imprimatur* are a declaration that a text is considered to be free of doctrinal or moral error. They do not necessarily imply agreement with opinions expressed by the author.

ISBN 0 905092 99 6
Cat. No. 3394

Origination by Joe Healy Typesetting, Dublin 2.
Printed in the Republic of Ireland by Genprint Limited, Dublin 3.

# Acknowledgements

The photographs on pages 4, 6, 14 are reproduced by courtesy of the Trustees of The National Gallery, London, and those on pages viii, 20, 28, 37, 44, 48 by kind permission of The Mansell Collection, London.

The Author and the Publisher are also grateful to the following for permission to quote copyright material in this book:
Fr Richard Loehrlein, S.M., for an extract from a private communication to the Author; Fr Vincent Couesnongle, O.P., for comment on paragraph 51 of *Marialis Cultus*; Fr Jonathan Fleetwood, O.P., Prior Provincial of the English Dominicans for translations of material by Dominic of Prussia from an unpublished MS by Fr Raymond Devas, O.P.; David McKay Co., Inc., New York, for an extract from *To see Peter* by Richard Baumann; The Rosary Apostolate, Dublin, for a quotation from *The Good News of The Rosary*; Rev. Gerard Irvine for material originally published in *The Rosary*; The Methodist Publishing House, London, for an extract from *Five for Sorrow, Ten for Joy* by J. Neville Ward.

While every effort has been made to contact holders of copyright on material quoted in this book, if any involuntary infringement of copyright has occurred the holder of such copyright is requested to contact the Publisher.

# Contents

# 1 The legend of the Rosary

*First time I heard the legend of the Rosary, I smiled and thought "how childish". But when I heard the scripture scholars of our time explain the importance of legend and myth and parable, I had a second think.*

*When you ask: "Is the story true?" you are asking the wrong question. What you should be inquiring about is: "What's the truth behind the legend?"*

The legend of the Rosary begins with St Dominic in the early thirteenth century, when the Christian foundation was being shaken by the Catharist or Albigensian heresy. These people claimed that the body and all material creation were evil. To this day you can find remainders of their thinking in the curious souvenirs from that part of Southern France where they flourished. One of them that comes to mind:

*Three things that rule and ruin a man:*
*Wine, women and wealth . . .*

The Catharist refused to drink wine for it was a symbol of life on which he turned his back. Woman, the life-bearer, was despised and marriage rejected. Wealth, property and all the external expressions of religion were played down. It was a strange mixture of puritanical asceticism, of opting out of society and of dabbling in

---

*Opposite*

***St Dominic, linked by tradition with the origins of the Rosary as it exists in the Catholic Church. This picture by Fra Angelico, one of his spiritual sons, shows Dominic who "spent the night speaking to God and the day speaking of God".***

***St Dominic is seldom seen with the beads in his hands, as are so many others. Rather, he is presented as a man of deep prayer or as a preacher, with the theme of his preaching shown in the background and a crowd of listeners before him fingering the beads.***

the occult. And the logical conclusion of the doctrine was to deny the possibility of the Word of God taking flesh in the womb of a woman.

What was needed was a powerful preaching to tell the world once more that God had "emptied himself", being born in the likeness of men; "become obedient unto death"; and that now "Jesus Christ is Lord, to the glory of God the Father" *(Philippians 2 : 6-11).* This message formed the core of Dominic's sermons and was the heart of the Rosary preaching. It could be summed up in the greeting of Gabriel: "Rejoice, so highly favoured – you shall bear a son." Son, Saviour, Sovereign, there in embroyo was the Rosary, with its triple division of joyful, sorrowful and glorious mysteries.

And so the legend runs. St Dominic was having but scant success in his preaching to the Albigenses, when one day Our Lady herself came to his rescue. "Wonder not," she said,

> that until now you have had such little fruit from your labours: you have spent them on a barren soil, not yet watered with the dew of divine grace. When God willed to renew the face of the earth he began by sending down the fertilising dew of the Angelic Salutation. Preach my Rosary composed of 150 Aves, and you will obtain an abundant harvest.

The legend pinpointed the fact that fallen man was unable to help himself, that woman lay under a strange curse and that the very earth itself was unfruitful until the Saviour came. "Gabriel" means "God is my strength" and his message means that "the heavens are opening" and the clouds are going to "drop down dew from above".

Mary is still like the grass, patient like the flower, and the April dew is to make her Queen of a new creation. Notice the stillness of Mary as captured by this unknown poet.

*He came all so still*
*Where his mother was,*
*As dew in April*
*That falleth on the grass.*

*He came all so still*
*To his mother's bower,*
*As dew in April*
*That falleth on the flower.*

*He came all so still*
*where his mother lay,*
*As dew in April*
*That falleth on the spray.*

Anonymous
– fifteenth century

What we do in the Rosary is to be still "as dew in April" and allow the same heavenly blessing to fall on us. In the Hail Mary, we are not very active. Rather we are surrendering to the Lord, allowing the waters of heaven to wash gently over us, to make us clean and fresh and alive. We have been the barren, withered earth. Now we stand where Mary stood and become part of the new creation.

*The wedding of Giovanni Arnolfini and Giovanna Cenami.*

# 2 *The evolution of the Rosary*

The picture with this chapter is one of the treasures of the National Gallery in London, and is known as "The Wedding of Arnolfini". Few of the thousands who stand before it each year would be aware of its witness to the development of the Rosary.

## Significant date

The work is by the Netherlands painter, Jan Van Eyck, who died in 1441. For our purposes the only date that matters is the one that appears over the convex mirror, with the inscription: *Johannes de eyck fuit hic: 1434* (Jan Van Eyck was present here: 1434). The strange manner of signing has led to the conclusion that what is portrayed here is marriage consent, with the artist signing his name as witness. Reflected in the mirror are two figures in addition to the reflection of the consenting parties. These are most likely Van Eyck himself and his assistant.

## Beads and mysteries

Much has been written about the bride and bridegroom; about the single lighted candle symbolising the presence of the Lord; about the small dog representing the fidelity of marriage; about the statuette (probably that of St Margaret of Antioch, patron of expectant mothers); and other details of the painting. Our study, however, is directed more to the mirror frame and the string of beads hanging by.

Close inspection reveals ten circlets in the frame, depicting the following scenes from the life of Christ: The Agony, The Capture, Christ before Pilate, The Scourging, Jesus carrying the Cross, The Crucifixion, The taking down from the Cross, The Burial, Christ in Limbo, and The Resurrection.

## Historical evidence

Here we have the elements of the Rosary as used by Catholics today. The fifteen mysteries arranged in a triple cycle of the life, death and resurrection of Jesus have not yet finally emerged, but the idea of mysteries linked with the use of beads is obvious enough.

*Detail from the* Wedding of Arnolfini
*The prayer-beads with the tassel, on the wall beside the mirror, is typical of the kind in other paintings of the time. These beads were often worn from a belt, the ending tassel or medallion taking the place of the present-day Crucifix.*

*The small designs around the mirror depict The Agony, The Capture, Christ before Pilate, The Scourging, Jesus carrying the Cross, The Crucifixion, The taking down from the Cross, The Burial, Christ in Limbo, and The Resurrection.*

It is one of the earliest records we have in which a high level of acceptance is given to such a devotion in Europe. By gracing the wall of this distinguished merchant, the Rosary would seem to be taken for granted as part of normal Christian piety.

Evolution

It is noteworthy that the beads do not have the same number as today, and that there are only ten mysteries at this mid-fifteenth century stage. We ought not to think of the Rosary arriving in the days of St Dominic (two hundred years earlier) as a finished product and spreading through Europe in one clearly identifiable package. The history of the evolution of the Rosary is one of great diversity of form. The first two hundred and fifty years after the death of Dominic in 1221 reveal no definite pattern, and it is indeed only a half-century later than this painting by Van Eyck that we have the first clearly established attempt at unity. Even then, we find evidence of tensions between strict uniformity and a more general kind of unity.

Modern times

This matter has considerable relevance in our times. We find the Roman authorities anxious to maintain the "normative Rosary" as formulated by Pope Pius V (1566-1572) while at the same time recommending "certain exercises of piety which take their inspiration from the Rosary", incorporating "Bible readings, homily, accompanied with silent pauses and emphasised with song", (par. 55 of *Marialis Cultus* published at Rome, February 1974).

Understandable fears

One can understand the natural fears of those who want "no interference with the existing form of the Rosary". They will remark: "Our Lady gave us the Rosary as we now know it through St Dominic, seven hundred years ago. You can't interfere with what Our Lady herself settled once and for all."

One must be sensitive to the feelings and the piety of people. Local leaders of Rosary societies will be the best judges of each situation. But it should be understood that the foregoing statement about Our Lady and St Dominic is not accurate and can lead to false conclusions. As Eithne Wilkins in her scholarly study, *The*

*Rose Garden Game,* remarks: ". . . the Rosary was not suddenly 'invented' or 'introduced', as rabbits were into Australia! It is more the story of a continuously evolving and living experience."

This does not mean that a Rosary leader should spring sudden changes upon any group. People pray best in the way they are sweetly moved to by the Holy Spirit. Techniques of prayer and changes that might disturb the quiet tranquility of contemplation are not to be indulged in. At the same time, it can help to see the Rosary not only as a beautiful form of prayer, but also as a general method of prayer. It should lead in some way to meditating on the whole riches of the scriptures, and even to going beyond meditation to the stillness and peace of resting in the divine presence.

Pope Paul VI

The words of Pope Paul VI in *Marialis Cultus* (par. 55) deserve serious consideration: "We desire that this worthy devotion should not be propagated in a way that is too *one-sided* or *exclusive.* The Rosary is an excellent prayer, but the faithful should feel *serenely free* in its regard. They should be drawn to its calm recitation by its *intrinsic appeal.*" (The emphasis in this quotation is mine.)

*Not one-sided* Is this not an invitation to see the many faces of the Rosary? Is it not a call to follow the prompting of the Holy Spirit, at least in private or small groups, meditating perhaps on other Gospel mysteries, e.g. the Baptism of the Lord, the Cana incident, or the mystery of the Eucharist? Is it not an indication that there can be different approaches to the Rosary?

*Serenely free* Perhaps we have exercised a kind of spiritual violence by expecting *all* to pray the Rosary. I am not quite sure how one reconciles this with certain of our crusading efforts. Prayer should be a loving relationship with our Father in heaven, not a matter of "you must . . ."

*Intrinsic appeal* We are being asked to pray the Rosary not because of a command or of some outside appeal, but rather from the very nature of the prayer itself.

Pope Paul would have had in mind what St Thomas Aquinas said: "Prayer not only gives glory to God, but provides nourishment and rejoicing for the soul itself." He would have been aware, too, of the many-splendoured spirituality which the Rosary provided through the centuries.

# 3 *Mantras and Meditation*

The Rosary has a many-splendoured history. It also has a geography. It is to be found in some form or other among Hindus, Buddhists, Muslims, and Jews.

Popular pamphleteers in Roman Catholic circles sometimes make statements like: "Wherever you see a Rosary, there you know you've got a Catholic. It is the badge of being a true child of the Church." On the other hand, sincere Protestants often have a holy fear of our beads, which they consider "papish superstition".

## Patrimony of all

The fact of the matter is that neither the Catholic pamphleteer nor the Protestant objector is quite accurate. Far from being the preserve of Roman spirituality, the practice of meditation while fingering beads, and the very name "Rosary" itself, are part of the spiritual patrimony of all mankind.

## Spiritual genocide

A study of the Rosary among the major religions of the world can benefit Catholics, apart altogether from allaying the fears of others. A word of caution, however: while learning from these usages, it must be stressed that approval is not thereby given to their theological implications. At present there is a vogue of Eastern cults, and many are misled into thinking they have found a substitute for their own Christian faith. With this caution, it may be worth looking at these mainstream religions, if only to realise that to do away with the beads would be to drag down a whole fabric of human culture. It would be little short of spiritual genocide.

## The Hindus

Pious Hindus use the beads to keep count of invocations to their gods, but also as a means of promoting contemplation. Much store is put on the beads themselves, and some can only be got from an "accomplished Yogi". There is an account of one old hermit exerting great physical energy in turning a large wheel with huge beads attached. The Rosary plays a part in the initiation of children to the cult of the Visnu, and there are collections of invocations used on such occasions, such as: "Homage to the adorable Rama", or "Adorable Krishna is my refuge".

### Mantra

The invocations quoted above are known as "mantras". While some of them are striking, it must be stressed that they are addressed to pagan gods: "Let us adore the divine Vivifier. May he enlighten our understanding." In Hindu usage, it is sometimes difficult to distinguish between the rosary as a religious thing and as a mere charm.

### Buddhist

In India, the Buddhist rosary does not seem to differ very much from Hindu. In Tibet, the word for telling the beads means literally "to purr like a cat". Contemplatives have always been attracted by the rhythmic hum of the cat, and have adopted cats as companions. One Irish monk even had a "Pangur Bán" (white Pangur cat).

The Eastern mentality has not been given to active thought as a help to meditation. It prefers the often meaningless sound or soothing repetition of a mantra as an aid to stillness. A favourite Buddhist mantra is "Hail, thou Jewel in the Lotus!", but others are more or less unintelligible even to the worshipper. On laying aside his Rosary, the Korean Buddhist repeats: "Oh! the thousand miles of emptiness, the place which is in the midst of the tens of hundred myriad miles of emptiness . . . eternal desert where the true Buddha exists. There is eternal existence with tranquil peace."

### Muslim

In Persia and India, the Rosary is called "tasbih", deriving from an Arabic word meaning "to praise" or "to exalt". The Prophet Mohammed attributed great merit to reciting the names of God and giving praise to Allah a hundred times in the morning and again in the evening.

From Egypt, comes the record of wakes for the dead with continuous recitation of the rosaries, punctuated with strong coffee (shades of old Irish customs . . . but with something stronger than coffee). At certain stages the prayer-leader asks aloud: "Have ye transferred the merit of your prayers to the soul of the deceased?" The reply is: "We have so transferred them, praise be God the Lord of all creatures!"

Jews and Greeks

Among the Jews, the rosary appears to have lost all religious significance. It was taken over by them from the Turks and Greeks. In Greek monasteries, a knotted cord or string of beads is used as part of the ecclesiastical garb. The laity also use this cord often simply as something to hold in the hand like "worry beads". It is known as a "kombologion" by the Greeks, and "chotki" by the Russians.

Comment

Many are worried about the inroads of Eastern religions, and in particular the practice of Transcendental Meditation by Christians today. Father Richard Loehrlein, S.M., an American priest working in Dublin writes:

> T.M. is advertised as a "scientific method of relaxation", but in fact it is the Hindu religion being taught in psychological language. No one receives a mantra without participating in the Hindu sacrifice called the *puja,* in which flowers, fruit and a white cloth are the offerings. Indian Christians regard the taking of a mantra in such circumstances as part of the Hindu religion.

One wonders why Christians, and Catholics in particular, spend large sums of money to learn these Eastern practices. Having looked at them even in this skimpy fashion, one notes that whatever good they may have is found in a higher and more efficacious way in the simple practice of our own Rosary. All the elements noted in them are to be found in the Christian Rosary, but in a more refined and exalted form:

1. Praise

The continued praise of God for the gift of Jesus his Son, and for all the gifts he has bestowed on Mary, the Queen of his creation: "Blessed art thou . . . and blessed is the fruit of your womb, Jesus."

2. Rhythm

The rhythmic sound of the Paters and Aves which still the mind and rest the heart with their old familiar phrases. They are heaven's own "mantra". They are far from meaningless sounds, and their very familiarity and precious association lift one out of depression and despair. We hesitate, indeed, to use the expression "mantra", which in the Hindu context signifies "charm" and is often used to cast a spell.

3. Meditation

It has always been part of the Christian and Jewish tradition that "with desolation is the whole land made desolate because there is no one who thinks in the heart" *(Jer 12:11)*. The essence of the Rosary is quiet thinking in the heart. Beginners in meditation will concentrate on each mystery and try to picture the scene and the message of the Lord. But those making progress in the way of mental prayer will use the Rosary to still the mind and rest the heart as they enter the presence of the true God and Father of men.

Many give up the Rosary because they feel they "cannot meditate." The fact is that, through the Rosary, they may have gone beyond the stage of meditation and entered the restful state of contemplative prayer.

One can give this a grand name like "being lost in the divine Absolute", or entering "the essence of all reality". But, praise God, thousands, maybe millions, of very ordinary Christians have found this experience for themselves through the rhythms of the Rosary, and the mysteries of the Gospel that are its soul.

# 4 *How to meditate*

*The world is too much with us*
*Late and soon;*
*Getting and spending*
*We lay waste our powers.*

We've got to stop that soul-drain! The first thing is to be convinced that meditation has a lot to offer and that, far from being an imposition, it is something that can be a joy. Let it be said that the Rosary provides a simple and effective method of meditation, combining all that is best of human culture and of the counsels of God.

The Rosary-meditation takes us out of the rat race of getting and spending, and helps concentrate our powers on the Lord. Busy executives have learned to sit quietly on the commuter train with the beads in their hands and their minds on the divine mysteries. Father Cussen, the Dominican who preached the Rosary all over Australia, tells of one fretful commuter looking over his paper at a fellow passenger who appears to be snoozing in the corner and saying: "O'Hara is a tiger for sleep", only to be told later: "O'Hara is not asleep. He's away with Jesus on the hills of Gallilee."

There is nothing so easy as to finger the rosary-beads and be in Gallilee or on Calvary, or in the upper room waiting for the Spirit, even while riding on bus or train, or standing in a queue.

## Ecumenical borrowing

In true ecumenical spirit, we can borrow from the riches of other traditions to help our meditation. Indeed, it is scarcely necessary to do anything but quote from other sources for this chapter, as there is such an abundance of literature and tapes now available on this theme.

## "Be still"

The first requirement for meditation is to be still: "Be still before the Lord, and wait for him" *(Ps 37:7)*. Being still, and waiting

14

for the Lord: there is the secret of prayer and of peace. The *New American Bible* puts it forcefully: "Leave it to the Lord . . ." It is a kind of letting go, and letting God! Psalm 131 invites us to rest like children in the arms of the Lord:

> *I have stilled and quieted my soul,*
> *Like a child quieted at its mother's breast* (Ps 131:2).

The very holding of the beads can induce this quietness, symbolising and summing up as it does the "Mother-and-child" scheme of salvation.

Carry no burden

"Take care not to carry burdens on the Sabbath day" said the prophet Jeremiah. The words applied literally (in *Jeremiah 17:21*) to the carrying of material burdens and to trading on the Sabbath. But in the deeper sense it is a command to come before the Lord with joy. If we wish to enter the rest of the Lord, we should cast aside fear and anxiety, whether it be about finance or family, about health, or anything else. In meditation, we cast aside the slave mind, and recognise that we are sons and heirs of the Father. We enter the house of the Lord with praise, celebrating a perpetual Sabbath in our hearts. We are to "Look to the Lord and be radiant" *(Ps 34:6)*.

Reflecting the radiance of the Lord

Here we find the fruit of meditation and its helpfulness to daily living. We learn to look to the Lord and become transformed. It is told of Moses that when he conversed with God on the mountain the people could see the radiance of God reflected on his face. So great was this glory that Moses had to cover his face with a veil.

---

*Opposite*

The Bible and the Beads
*Detail from a work by Rogier van der Weyden (1399-1464). The central theme of the painting would most likely have been a scene from the life of Christ. These two side characters are depicted contemplating the scene. The man with the beads and the woman with the Gospels are delicately harmonised to give a fine understanding of the true nature of the Rosary which weds the Book and Beads together.*

This was what St Paul was referring to when he told the Corinthians that: "All we, with unveiled faces, reflecting the glory of the Lord, are being changed into his likeness from one degree of glory to another; for this comes from the Lord who is the Spirit" *(2 Cor 3:18).*

You are being changed!

One could keep that verse before the mind's eye in the Rosary. As you look at Jesus in each mystery, you are "being changed into his likeness". All you have to do is rest in his presence; to appreciate the fact that he sees you, that he knows you, that he accepts you just are you are.

You do not contemplate him as a dim distant figure of the past. He is before you right now and, wonder of wonders, he does not leave you as you are. By his spirit he changes you. He transforms you into his very own likeness.

One degree of glory to another

Oh blessed secret of the Rosary! When used as intended by God, it removes the veil from our eyes and opens us to "the glory of the Lord".

Do not be diverted from this "looking to the Lord" by the multiplicity of mysteries and by the vocal prayers of the Rosary. A lot of things in this book are for the purpose of preaching and preparation. When the actual time of prayer comes, it should be blissfully simple. There should be no strained searching after thoughts or mental images. Attend to the words, if you feel drawn that way. Concentrate on the historical events or the meaning of the mysteries, if the Spirit so moves you. But very likely you will let the Lord do the leading and the transforming. You will simply reflect his glory.

Use of the Mary-Jesus "Mantra"

It is at this stage that something like the Eastern mantra helps, or what the monk Cassian called "the poverty of a single word". One word like "Mary", or the holy name of "Jesus", may gather all your thoughts and desires into one still sound. Or you may find peace in the rhythmic balance of the Ave: *("Blessed* are thou . . . *blessed* is the fruit of your womb . . .") Or again, you may whisper gently: "Come, Lord Jesus" by way of spiritual communion with Jesus in these sacred mysteries. As you begin the Lord's Prayer, you may just breathe the utterance of Christ himself: "Abba – Father". For a person who has already prepared his soul by reading the Scriptures or by listening to a homily, a single phrase may span the whole panorama of the Rosary-landscape.

When you find a phrase or a word that speaks to your soul, you may stay with it and carry it right through the Rosary in deep, restful, meditation. The "Jesus-clause" will be found particularly helpful in this exercise. (See chapter 8.)

The very simplicity and seeming monotony of oft-repeated words in the Rosary, far from being boring, is the key to meditation. Because of the familiarity of well-worn paths, one is open and free to let the Spirit breathe where it will.

### Setting the mood

Meditation of this kind runs deeper than words or thoughts. It sets a mood that leads on to the prayer of affection and of union. In the Christian context, the Holy Spirit joins with the spirit of man in a divine conspiracy that shows itself in the gifts and fruits of the Spirit.

### Renewal

Here lies the meaning of renewal. It is not the Rosary that requires change or renewal. It is we, by the power of the Spirit, who are being transformed and made new, as we advance from one degree of glory to another along this simple way of meditation and contemplation.

# 5 *The Gospel on its knees*

Look up the Gospel text for the Feast of the Rosary . . . I imagine you'll find it as you expected: the story of the Angel Gabriel coming to Mary.

But if you can unearth a Dominican Missal such as was in use when I entered the Order in 1949, you'll discover quite a different story. The text may surprise you. It is *Luke 8, verses 1 to 10,* the theme of which is the preaching of the Good News:

> *Jesus journeyed through towns and villages, preaching and bringing the good news of the kingdom of God . . . He said: a sower went out to sow his seed . . .*
>
> *To you it has been given to know the secrets of the Kingdom . . .* (Privileged Mass of the Rosary).

Revolutionary approach

Here we are at the heart of the traditional understanding of the Rosary, as *a method of preaching the Gospel,* of making known the mysteries of the Kingdom of Heaven. It is significant that thirteenth- and fourteenth-century art, while depicting many other figures with strings of beads in their hands, consistently shows Dominic with the book of the Gospels. We are told that he knew the Letters of St Paul by heart.

It was in line with this tradition that the International Rosary Congress held in Rome in 1976 insisted that what we are to preach is not the Rosary itself, but the Gospel *by means of the Rosary.* This may seem a small point, but it has revolutionary effects in the building up of a Rosary spirituality and apostolate.

Original inspiration

Pope Paul VI, in *Marialis Cultus,* paid tribute to those who have been "uncovering the original inspiration and driving force behind the original structure of the Rosary". He observed that the division of the mysteries of the Rosary into three parts not only adheres strictly to the chronological order, but reflects the original proclamation of the faith and sets forth the mystery of Christ in the very way in which it is seen by St Paul in the celebrated "hymn" of the *Letter to the Philippians* . . . self-emptying (kenosis), death, and exaltation *(2:6-11).*

1. *He emptied himself, taking the form of a servant, being born in the likeness of men.*
   (The Joyful Mysteries)
2. . . . *obedient unto death, even death on a cross* . . .
   (The Sorrowful Mysteries)
3. *Jesus Christ is Lord, to the glory of God the Father.*
   (The Glorious Mysteries)

When during the Rome Congress, the question came up as to why we should be confined to the traditional fifteen mysteries of the Rosary, we were told that the triple division according to the "Paschal Mystery", representing the fundamental Christian evangelisation, should be maintained. However, other mysteries could be included. But as far as possible they should be built around the central core of *joyful, sorrowful,* and *glorious.*

"Certain exercises . . ."

Paragraph 51 of *Marialis Cultus* gives ample room for experiment in this field, when it refers to "certain exercises of piety which take their inspiration from the Rosary". The Holy Father speaks of what might be called "a little liturgy of the Word" built around "meditation on the mysteries, repetition of the Ave . . . in the context of Bible readings, illustrated with a homily, accompanied by silent pauses and emphasised with song". "We are happy to know", adds Pope Paul, "that such practices have helped to promote a more complete understanding of the spiritual riches of the Rosary itself, and have served to restore esteem for its recitation among youth associations."

Commenting on this paragraph, Father Vincent de Couesnongle, Master of the Dominican Order, said:

> It would be unfaithful to this exhortation to ignore it systematically under the pretext that it cannot interest the preachers of the true Rosary. To apply this teaching of Pope Paul is not to enter into competition with the Rosary. It is, on the contrary, teaching the faithful to pray the Rosary better, and reveal its true nature.

Challenge of youth

Reproaching those who would find refuge in the notion that young people today are not interested in prayer, he added:

> Young people have a new desire for true, silent, and shared prayer. This is a privileged period for us. What are we promoters of the Rosary doing to draw these young people?

For the comfort of anyone thinking this is some new-fangled idea, let me quote from chapter 18 of *Le Triple Rosaire* by Pére Bernard, the sixteenth-century Dominican of Toulouse, concerning the preacher of the Rosary: "He must be a man of *freedom of spirit*, choosing well the themes of this devotion and the virtues enshrined in the mysteries." Three degrees of freedom are called for.

> *Three Freedoms of the Spirit*
> He must be free to follow the movement of the Spirit, whose instrument he is. If, for example, during his prayer time, he is inspired to preach a particular message, he should feel free to do so, not stifling the movement of the Spirit who is the soul of preaching.
>
> The second freedom of the preacher is that, when having prepared what he should say, in the course of his sermon, the Holy Spirit gives him new light or impulse, he should even then feel free to follow this direction. There are many who just cannot depart from what they have so carefully prepared; but we speak of those who are ready to follow the movement of grace when it offers them new light. The preacher who lacks this freedom is in danger of losing much grace and hindering the blessing which God wishes to bestow.
>
> The third freedom is to be ready at all times to preach, even when there is not much time for preparation, according to the word of God: "as the Spirit gives you utterance". Such preachers are in a continuous state of preparedness, and are filled with zeal and knowledge.

The preacher who has these three freedoms sees the needs of the Church and responds to them as moved by the Holy Spirit. He speaks with power and produces much fruit.

---

*Opposite*

*St Jerome in the desert is often shown using beads as an aid to contemplation. This is in keeping with the many devout souls who, through the centuries, have coupled their love of the Scriptures with praying on beads.*

Background

From the evidence available, it seems clear that this freedom for the preacher of the Rosary, was reflected in a freer style of Rosary for the congregation. From the vast collections of surviving manuals compiled by the Friars Preachers, we see that they did not confine themselves to the stock fifteen mysteries but encompassed the whole range of the Gospels.

A good example of what is meant is the sermon set down for the miracle of the woman with the issue of blood: "If only I can touch the tassel of his garment, I shall be made well." The preacher exhorts his hearers to reach for their Rosaries as if they were the tassel of the Lord's dress, not for any power in the beads or in the tassel but as faith-links with the healing power of Jesus himself.

When the head of the Dominicans today remarks that "We must surpass a slavish, material approach to the Rosary . . .", he is simply calling us to rediscover our former freedom in the Spirit.

# 6 *The "Jesus clauses"*

One of the simplest ways of highlighting the mystery of Jesus in the Rosary is to use the "Jesus clauses". Paragraph 46 of *Marialis Cultus* treats of the custom of "adding to the name of Jesus in each Hail Mary a reference to the mystery being contemplated . . . This was done to help contemplation and to make the mind and the voice act in unison."

There is nothing novel in this suggestion. It is, in fact, a recall to an ancient practice, and there are parts of Europe where the custom has never died out.

Dominic of Prussia

One of the best-known examples comes from Dominic of Prussia, (1384-1460). For these, I am indebted to Father Raymund Devas, O.P., of the English Dominican Province, from whose translation I quote:

> Hail Mary, full of grace, the Lord is with thee, blessed are thou among women, and blessed is the fruit of your womb, Jesus Christ, whom at the word of the Angel thou didst conceive, by the Holy Ghost, Amen.
>
> . . . Jesus Christ, whom thou didst suckle at thy virgin breasts.
>
> . . . Jesus Christ, who gavest light to the blind, cleansed the lepers, cured the paralytics
>
> . . . Jesus Christ, who on the day of Pentecost didst send down the Holy Spirit.

Dominic of Prussia gives fifty clauses in all, and while he ranges over the full panorama of the Gospel he manages to cover our present series of fifteen mysteries.

I believe these particular clauses would be somewhat cumbersome to our ears, and would require a book to say them, giving rise as they did to the expression "reading the Rosary". But one thing they, and other such clauses, reveal is that the Rosary meant very different things to different people according to the stage of their spiritual growth.

The following examples for the "perfect" or "contemplative" souls are rather beautiful:

Hail Mary . . . fruit of thy womb, Jesus:

who shed blood and water from the side – may we be redeemed in this blood and find shelter in his wounds.

Jesus:

who willed to remain three days resting in the tomb – may he bury us in the earth of a quiet heart and a still conscience.

Jesus:

who filled the disciples with the gifts of the Holy Spirit – may he fill us with the fire of love, the spirit of fear, and of knowledge, and of strength.

Jesus:

who lives and reigns for ever – may we too reign with Him for ever.

The above Clauses are taken from a work published at Cologne in 1516 (Vatican Library, RG, Teol., V.4417).

De Montfort

De Montfort, in *The Secret of Mary,* gives his own list, which has the appearance of having been pruned to a nicety by the practical findings of an experienced preacher:

At the 1st Decade . . . "Jesus incarnate";
At the 2nd ,, . . . "Jesus sanctifying";
At the 3rd ,, . . . "Jesus born in poverty";
At the 4th ,, . . . "Jesus sacrificed";
At the 5th ,, . . . "Jesus, Saint among saints";
At the 6th ,, . . . "Jesus in His agony";
At the 7th ,, . . . "Jesus scourged";
At the 8th ,, . . . "Jesus crowned with thorns";
At the 9th ,, . . . "Jesus carrying His Cross";
At the 10th ,, . . . "Jesus crucified";
At the 11th ,, . . . "Jesus risen from the dead";
At the 12th ,, . . . "Jesus ascending to heaven";
At the 13th ,, . . . "Jesus filling Thee with the Holy Spirit";
At the 14th ,, . . . "Jesus raising Thee up";
At the 15th ,, . . . "Jesus crowning Thee".

Communion with Jesus

It might be well to remember that these clauses were introduced at a time when the Hail Mary ended with, and built up to a climax in, the holy name of Jesus. To gain the full fruit of the clause it seems essential to savour it for some moments, and not to rush into the "Holy Mary . . ." response. The whole point of the exercise is to make of the Angel's greeting a communion with the Saviour, Jesus, to truly find rest in his name, to open ourselves to receive him as Mary did.

In *The Good News of The Rosary,* ten "Jesus clauses", mainly from scripture, are given for each mystery, but this is simply to allow for personal choice, e.g.

*The Five Joyful Mysteries*

| | |
|---|---|
| Annunciation: | Jesus, given to each one of us. |
| Visitation: | Jesus, filling Elizabeth with the Holy Spirit. |
| Nativity: | Jesus, first-born of all creation. |
| Presentation: | Jesus, revealing the secret thoughts of many. |
| Finding: | Jesus, hearing and asking questions. |

*The Five Sorrowful Mysteries*

| | |
|---|---|
| Agony: | Jesus, whose sweat became like drops of blood. |
| Scourging: | Jesus, by whose wounds we are healed. |
| Crowning: | Jesus, rejected by men. |
| Carrying Cross: | Jesus, led like a lamb to the slaughter. |
| Crucifixion: | Jesus, pierced by a lance. |

*The Five Glorious Mysteries*

| | |
|---|---|
| Resurrection: | Jesus, the redemption of our bodies. |
| Ascension: | Jesus, appearing in the presence of God on our behalf. |
| Descent of Spirit: | Jesus, pouring out his Spirit on all flesh. |
| Assumption: | Jesus, we shall see him and be radiant. |
| Coronation: | Jesus, for he is Lord. |

# 7 *Rejoice daughter*

Why not leave us the simple Gospel on its knees? Why complicate matters with the repetition of Paters and Aves?

The Spirit blows where it wills, so naturally there will be times when all we want to do is to sit and say nothing. St Catherine, the mystic of Siena, with her deep common sense, says that while the repetition of the vocal prayers is an aid to concentration, the higher purpose is to open the soul to God's Spirit. "And when this happens," she adds, "the soul, overcome by the movement of the Spirit, should cease from saying . . . and just rest in the Lord" *(Letters).*

While the full Rosary contains 150 Hail Marys (the number is based on the 150 Psalms of the Bible), the whole point of the exercise is that in the quiet, rhythmic repetition we learn to rest in the name of Jesus which is central to the prayer. For, strictly speaking, this is not so much a prayer as a scriptural greeting announcing the good news of the Incarnation: "Rejoice, so highly favoured! The Lord is with you."

Rejoice: a creative command

It should be noted that the word "Rejoice", on Gabriel's lips, was not the banal form of greeting in normal Greek usage. It was, rather, a singular salutation evocative of all the messianic promises. It was one of the key words of the Old Testament that spilt right over into the New. It was, in fact, one of the royal commands that went to the making of the new covenant between God and man in the person of Jesus.

It is not a first joy but "re-joy" to the world, and it fits in with that whole scheme of re-creative words that fill the pages of scripture: "rebuild, restore, repeople, return, repay, redeem, relieve, retrieve, refresh, replant". All these themes are fulfilled in the new people of God and in a particular way in the new Daughter of Zion.

*Rejoice heartily, O daughter of Zion,*
*Shout for joy, O daughter of Jerusalem.*

Or, again, we think of the Zephaniah promises to Jerusalem fulfilled in Mary and flowing over on all true sons and daughters of Zion.

*Shout for joy, daughter of Zion . . .*
*The Lord God is in your midst, a mighty saviour:*
*He will rejoice over you with gladness,*
*and renew you in his love.*
*He will sing joyfully over you*
*As one sings at festivals.*
(Zephaniah 3:17)

That must surely be one of the high-water marks of the flood of divine love poured out on humanity. And this is what greeted Mary's ears when Gabriel cried: "Rejoice . . . the Lord is in your midst." (In the original text it is the same word as: "in your womb".) We, who take up the word of God's messenger, make bold to enter these flood waters of joy, to be renewed ourselves in the divine love.

As I learn to rejoice, God takes over more and more in my life. Every time I hear the words "hail" or "rejoice", I seem to hear the roar of mighty waters, the rush of pentecostal winds, the loud shout of praising song. Heaven and earth resound with loud acclamation. And God himself is singing joyfully for me, as one sings at festivals, as he renews me in his love.

IC XC

# 8 *Full of grace: high favour*

Gabriel did not call the Virgin by her name. He gave her a title, or described her as the one "highly favoured" by God. The original text makes it clear that Mary is full of grace *because* she has been and is being filled from the living source of grace, which is the divine favour "freely bestowed on us in the beloved" *(Ephesians 1:6).* The Greek wording points to the Trinity and lights up the whole nature of grace as a free gift of God. This should remove any fear some might have of an expression like "full of grace" being applied to Mary.

One can be misled by the English text: "favoured" points to a past condition, and critics of Mary may say: "Fine, God favoured her in the past but that's over now." But the Greek has a two-fold past tense unknown to English grammar: the *aorist* which is a kind of "full-stop" past, and the *perfect* which is the one used here by Luke, implying not only a past condition, but an on-going reality as if to say: "Rejoice, for you have been, and still are being favoured . . ." So when called to pray like this, we are being invited to identify with God's own rejoicing. He still rejoices over his people, personified in Mary. And we are called to enter into this land where God himself is singing as on festivals *(Zephaniah 3).*

Mary's response

While grace is indeed a free bestowal or gift, it does imply a response. The divine favour does not overpower but empowers for mission. Mary laid her spirit completely open to the conspiracy between the Spirit of God and the spirit of man by saying "Yes" to the whole Christ. I'm thinking not only of the whole *physical*

---

*Opposite*

*Here is evidence of the slow development of the Rosary. This is Andrea Gallerani of Siena, shown as a deeply contemplative soul combining meditation on the Passion with the use of beads. We know that this man practised the "Paternoster" type of Rosary, as did St Catherine of the same city. The artist portrays Andrea pausing in the recitation of his vocal prayers to gaze in silent contemplation at the Crucified.*

life-style of Jesus, but of the whole *mystical* person that we call the Body of Christ, or the Church. Mary said "Yes" not only to Christ, the Head of that Body, but to *all* the members. Were it not so, notes St Augustine, she would have mothered a monster.

As members of Christ, we have been overshadowed by the Spirit, and brought forth through Mary's consent. "Thus", adds Augustine, "we are in this life, carried in the womb of Mary, and are not fully born until the day of our death . . . that being why we speak of the death of the saints as their birthday." We do not ask Mary to become our Mother. She has been given that office of mothering the whole Christ from the start. We merely acknowledge a divine plan, by making our own and accepting the high favour bestowed on each of us, who in Christ and by the power of the Spirit are carried by her.

### To be whole

To be whole people, we must be continually returning to this conception-point of the Annunciation. Wounds carried over from a pre-natal condition, hurts sustained as children, or rejection experienced in later life, all these are the concern of the Christ-Mother who continues to say "Yes" to us as she said "Yes" to Jesus. If the natural mother plays so large a part in both hurt and healing, it is hard to see how any valid Christian healing ministry could leave out the role of Mary.

### Fill the empty spaces

The first part of the Hail Mary, then, is not only a lesson in prayer. It teaches us about life, about God's renewing healing love.

*Lord God,*
*We praise and thank you*
*for the marvels*
*you have done for Mary, your handmaid.*
*We rejoice*
*that you are still*
*in the midst of us*
*and that through her*
*you give Jesus*
*to the waiting world,*
*to fill up the empty spaces*
*and renew us*
*in your love.*

# 9 *Blest are you . . . blest is the fruit . . .*

*Blest are you . . . blest is the fruit . . .*
(Luke 1:42)

Even in a translation, the rhythm is beautiful, and ideally suited to induce quiet contemplation. There is a sense of balance and proportion. Mary's blessedness is set in the right context, as happens later when the woman in the crowd cries out: "Blessed is the womb that bore you" *(Luke 11:27).*

## When two are one

It reminds me of my architect colleague, Father Bonaventure Leahy, O.P., who solved the construction problem of Mary in relation to the Blessed Sacrament. He set the image of Our Lady above and behind the tabernacle gazing in adoration at the Eucharistic Presence. It was easy to kneel in that Church and, with one simple glance, observe the meaning of: "Blessed are you . . . blessed is the fruit of your womb." The rhythm of the words is clearly seen to build up to a climax in the name and in the presence of Jesus: "Hail Mary . . . the Lord is with you! . . . and blessed is the fruit of your womb, Jesus."

## Scriptural backing

But the scriptural backing to this rhythm is more important: The words in Luke's narrative are solemnly introduced with the remark:

*Elizabeth was filled with the Holy Spirit,*
*and cried out in a loud voice* (Luke 1 : 42).

The "loud cry" is the cry of the Spirit witnessing to the inspired word. We can take these words from the lips of Elizabeth and be assured that they are God's own words. We know, too, that they are prophetic words, being confirmed by Mary in her own fulness of the Spirit when, in one breath, she rejoices in God and declares that "all ages shall call me blessed" *(Luke 1 : 47-48).*

Objection answered

At this stage, one might recall the oft-quoted passage of Luke 11:27-28

> *. . . a woman in the crowd called out, "Blest is the womb that bore you and the breasts that nursed you!"*

and the reply of Jesus:

> *Blest rather are they who hear the word of God and keep it.*

Some have held that Jesus was objecting to her being called blest, and the English "rather" might appear to lend substance to the case. The Greek original, however, uses the word "menoun" which has two meanings, one negative, the other positive: (1) a denial, or placing of opposition; (2) yes, and further still . . .

Americans use the word "rather", with a clearly positive note of praise and commendation: "Would you like to come for a drive?" "Yes, rather!" The Phillips translation has Jesus answering: "True for you, and furthermore . . . Spencer translates: "Yes indeed . . . blessed are they . . ." The French Dominican, Lagrange, sounds this same positive praise-note: "Bien mieux . . ." which in English means pretty much the same as "Yes, indeed!" So that, far from playing her down, Jesus is commending his mother as one who, in a special way, is blest for the keeping of his word.

Clearly, Jesus would not have denied the goodness of his Mother, who in this very area has already been twice noted for "pondering the word in her heart" *(Luke 1 : 19, 51)*. So we are left with the conclusion that these words of the "Hail Mary", spoken by Elizabeth under the influence of the Holy Spirit, are reinforced by Jesus himself.

It doesn't matter if you still want to maintain that the whole point of this text is to stress the spiritual relationship with Jesus arising from keeping his word. For Mary, the Daughter of Zion, is right out in front in her zeal for hearing God's word and shaping her life by it. After all, her word at Cana as the first red wine of the new covenant flowed, was: "Whatever, he says, do ye . . ."

# 10 *Mother of my Lord*

*Who am I, that the mother of my Lord should come to me?*
(Luke 1:43)

In every mystery Mary comes as Queen-Mother on royal visitation, carrying Jesus to those who would open to receive him as Elizabeth did. To taste the full flavour of the title "Mother of my Lord" one must realise that in the Jewish royal household the mother-figure was more significant that that of wife. There could be many wives, but one would be "more equal than others", she whose son was to succeed to the throne. She was specially dear to the Lord King as her son was the "Lord-to-be" When he came to the throne, his mother would be given special status and often great power. This was natural enough in a society of polygamy, where none of the royal wives enjoyed security or power until her son's succession was established.

Bathsheba and Solomon

Take the story of Bathsheba, who at first had been the object of King David's lustful desire. She had been used, victimised, thrown aside and, together with her son Solomon, classed as criminal. But she was rescued from this wretched condition by reminding David of his oath: "My Lord, you swore to me, your handmaid . . . that my son Solomon should reign after you and sit upon your throne" *(1 Kings 1:17).*

More mother than wife

As wife of David, Bathsheba bows to the floor in homage. But in the next chapter, as mother of the Lord King, we read:

> *. . . the king stood to meet her and paid her homage. Then he sat down upon his throne, and a throne was provided for the king's mother, who sat at his right.*
> *There is one small favour I would ask of you", she said, "Do not refuse me."*
> *"Ask it, my mother", the king said, "for I will not refuse you . . ."*
> (1 Kings 2:19-20)

## Pagan borrowing

It would appear that the Jews borrowed the "Mother-of-the-Lord" theme, together with the position of King, from the surrounding pagan world. According to one African custom, still practised, the young chief-to-be spends fifteen days being prepared by his mother. On the day of his installation, the mother rides ahead. At his solemn enthronement, she sits near him and prompts him.

## Marian implications

All of this has implications for Elizabeth's exclamation: "Who am I, that the Mother of my Lord should come to me?" Elizabeth, like her contemporaries, would have known how the mothers of Kings were prominent in the royal genealogies. And Luke, writing at a later date when the Lordship of Jesus had been recognised, may well have set down these words as a reflection of the early Christian community on the singular blessedness of Mary.

## Highly favoured

So we return to the source of Marian devotion. The favour and the power of this New Testament Queen-Mother are very real. But they are entirely given, the "free gift in the beloved" *(Ephesians).* Elizabeth, filled with the Holy Spirit, affirms God's choice of Mary and, with her baby leaping in her womb, invites all generations to make this same "leap for joy".

It is good to see a Methodist writer, Neville Ward, in *Five for Sorrow, Ten for Joy,* delighting at the ability to rejoice over the favour God grants to one of his privileged creatures. This indeed is the ground for true prayer of petition, leaping out of our self-centred world into the new world of praise. Praise God for "the great things he has done" *(Luke 1:49).* Praised be Jesus, the Lord! And blest be you, Mary, among all women, for you are the "Mother of my Lord"!

# *11 Pray for us sinners*

I was surprised to learn from other Christians that, while they had no objection to the first part of the "Hail Mary", they could not accept the second half. An esteemed Church of Ireland minister explained: "Our difficulty is about asking Mary to pray *for* us. There is no warranty in scripture for that practice."

## Two histories

The second part of this prayer, "Holy Mary, Mother of God, pray for us sinners now and at the hour of our death", has a totally different history to the first scriptural-greeting section. The earliest known English version of the "Holy Mary pray for us . . ." dates from 1493. Only in 1568, with the Reform of the Breviary, do we get an official version of the full prayer.

## Do not be afraid!

I can well understand how a prayer-form with such a late start might not appeal to some people. But then, "not appealing" is one thing. "Being frightened of" or "objecting to" is another. Catholics make no claim that this part of the Rosary derives from the Gospels as the first part does. It is simply a matter of a people's response in faith to a scriptural theme. The practice is enhanced by the fact that the response was built up over the centuries, and confirmed by the Church's teaching authority under the movement of the Holy Spirit. Moreover, one can still pray the Rosary as it was said for at least the first four centuries: a contemplative sharing in the Gospel using only the Angel's salutation. Many are doing just that at the present time, particularly when the "Jesus clauses" are used.

But to return to the objections. A Presbyterian remarked: "Of course we honour Mary, the Mother of the Word made flesh. It's just that we don't believe in reaching out to the dead. We honour Mary and all the saints for what the Lord did through them while they were on earth, but they cannot help us, nor can we reach them now that they have entered into their rest."

### Old Testament influence

Might I suggest that much of this view stems from Old Testament thinking, which had a pretty vague understanding of life after death, if indeed it really believed in any worthwhile after-life existence at all. Due, too, to pagan abuses and witchcraft there was a ban on communication with the dead.

### Good News of Jesus

With the Good News of Jesus, the concept of the dead took on a new dimension. Those who die in God's favour are more alive than any of us. In Christ, they are the most living of all members of the Communion of Saints. And we are encouraged to make friends with them here and now, so that later on they may "receive us into eternal dwellings" *(Luke 1:69).*

### Authority of the saints

Those who have won the victory are far from sitting in stately isolation from the "poor banished children of Eve". According to the Book of Revelation, they have been given "authority over the nations" *(Rev. 2:26)*, and they lift up "vessels of gold filled with aromatic spices, which are the prayers of God's people" *(Rev. 5:8).*

### All prayer is to God

It must not be thought that in the strict sense we offer our prayers to the saints or to Mary. All Christian prayer is directed to the Most Holy Trinity, and in Jesus we go directly to the Father through the power of the Holy Spirit. But there is nothing in scripture to prevent us going to holy people, either on earth or in heaven, to seek their intercession, remembering that it is the Christ in us that reaches out to the Christ in them, "for the flesh is of no avail" but "faith working through love" *(Gal. 5:6).*

# 12 *The three ages of the Rosary*

De Montfort set out three series of Rosary meditations: "for those who have only reached the stage of active contemplation, for those in the state of affective prayer, and for those quietly resting in the presence of God." For him the Rosary was a Jacob's ladder and souls might be on any level, or moving about from one prayer-level to another.

In this, De Montfort readily admitted that he was following the well established Dominican tradition. He would most likely have been familiar with the studies of Pére Bernard of Toulouse, to whom we have already referred. The latter speaks of "three ages of the Rosary", or three stages of Rosary mental prayer, apart altogether from concern with the vocal level: "The meditated Rosary for beginners, the Rosary of the affections for proficients, and the Rosary of union with God for the perfect." The following is a summary of his teaching on each of these areas.

## The Rosary of meditation

> At this stage we engage in serious reflection on the mysteries of the Rosary, in order to know, love and imitate the virtues of Jesus and Mary. No need to be frightened of the idea of meditation. The merchant meditates seriously his business, seeking ways of profit; the student meditates on his studies; while even the wicked meditates evil in his heart. Nothing more is required than goodwill and the aid of the Holy Spirit, together with some simple method.

## The Rosary of affection

Father Bernard then treats of the discernment needed to know when a soul is moving into the stage of intimacy with God, and so looking to the Lord more as friend than servant.

> The Rosary now becomes simpler and more profound. One makes acts of love, adoration, thanks, and petition; one listens and praises following the attraction of the moment. There may be darkness, one prays: "Lord, open my lips and my tongue shall declare your praise." There may be heaviness , one prays: "Heal me, Lord, for I have sinned against you."

The Mocking of Jesus *by Fra Angelico*

*It has been commented that Fra Angelico, the greatest painter of St Dominic and one of his sons in religion, never showed his master with the beads. We have many times stated in this book that contemplation, and not the beads, is the significant Dominican contribution to the Rosary. Mary is on no pedestal here. She is deep in contemplation of the Passion of her Son, with one hand holding her heavy head and the other extended in greeting to St Dominic who is reading the account in the Scriptures. It bears out the twentieth-century greeting of Mary in the Fatima appearances: "Keep me company, meditating on these mysteries."*

*This is a picture of the theology of the Rosary, showing the three elements harmoniously combined: the central mystery of Jesus:; the mystery of Mary, who treasures these things in her heart; and the mystery of myself, reading, pondering, praying.*

Like de Montfort, several centuries later, the author is conscious of the fact that some might at this stage abandon the Rosary. He advises that "one should pause in the recitation of the private Rosary and follow the lead of the Holy Spirit, taking it up at a later stage". He is concerned about the manner in which certain souls have been forced to remain in crude straight-jackets unsuited to their present stage of Rosary prayer.

This sixteenth-century Dominican master of the Rosary chooses his words with a fine balance, as will be recognised by those who may have agonised their way through these seasons of prayer.

### The Rosary of union

Addressing himself to directors and members of all Rosary fraternities, Father Bernard continues:

> Embrace then, devout souls, this Confraternity, in such fashion that those who pray the Rosary with a high degree of simple contemplation be not constrained to make complicated meditations, for that would be to pay their spiritual debts in silver, when they should be trading in gold!
>
> What I wish to stress is that a person who has arrived at a high degree of contemplation and unitive prayer would find meditation as such almost impossible. Having arrived at a passive kind of prayer, and already receiving the fruits of the Rosary, he is no longer helped by that searching which is peculiar to meditation. He must use the talent God has given him in restful prayer, applying it for the intentions of the fraternity.
>
> This kind of prayer is often compared to that of an infant asleep on its mother's breast, or like the drop of water lost in the ocean. One is lost in God – it may be an active or passive state, or a mixture of both, demanding purity of heart and the quieting of the passions.

### Personal experience

I believe that many people find themselves in this state after many years of practice in the Rosary, but fear they may not be praying well. They say: "I can no longer ponder the mysteries. I get lost, and before I know where I am, the Rosary is over."

One has only to look at such people to know that, if they are lost, they are lost in God. St Bernadette didn't know the names of the mysteries, yet she was wrapt to "the seventh heaven" as she knelt at the Grotto fingering the beads and murmuring the Aves. There is a stage beyond mere recitation or meditation, when one just rests before the Father.

Practical advice

Addressing himself once more to the members of the Rosary fraternity, Father Bernard says:

> Keep yourself in the presence of God, listening rather than speaking, quieting even thoughts and affections and all discursive meditation. You are no longer listening to the preacher, the director, or the holy books, but hearing God in the depths of your heart; for he speaks more effectively, more sweetly and more intelligently than any of these. God knows better the proper times and dispositions.

The author does not deny the need for preaching and meditation and study but he does insist that, at the actual time of praying the Rosary, a person in this state leaves aside all anxiety about carefully worked out mental images or desires. "These things" he says,

> dispose us for the Divine presence, but at prayer-time they no longer occupy the forefront of our minds.
>
> The preaching, the books, the meditation, have helped you, dear Rosarian, on your way, but now you must direct yourself to God alone, no longer striving to figure things out in the mind or stir up the affections. This work has already been done; now you are invited to rest in the Lord himself.
>
> Imagine a King who summons his two sons to reveal to them the secrets of his heart. One passes quickly through the ante-rooms to hasten to the throneroom; the other dallies on the way looking at the works of art, and never reaches the King. How much better to see the King than to be dazzled by his treasures.

Many of those called to be contemplatives in the Rosary act like this second son. Their Rosary should be one of simple union, but they weary themselves in the labour of meditation. Having mounted by this ladder, there is no need to drag it with them into the throne-room of God . . . but just run to him and rest in his presence.

And so, with a final word of encouragement, Father Bernard says.

> Freely, then, enter into this Brotherhood of the Mother of God, and you will increase your merits, gain many indulgences, and share in the prayers of all the members and of the whole Dominican Order; and win the favour of the Queen of the Most Holy Rosary.

Special note

In a note for people obliged to pray a certain number of Rosaries, in particular members of the Perpetual Rosary Society, Pére Bernard remarks:

> Those who do not wish to leave their practice of the simple presence of God and their prayer of union, may spend their Rosary Hour by simply applying their accustomed prayer for the intentions of the Rosary Hour. They should say one Ave at the beginning and one at the end for this purpose. When it happens that they are not drawn to say the full Rosary during the time allotted to them, they may say it in parts at various other times.

Fresh impetus

There is nothing particularly new about all this teaching. But to find it all set out in a large manual for directors of the Rosary Confraternities in the sixteenth century should give a fresh impetus to the Rosary brothers and sisters of our time. It also helps us to understand why Our Lady should come to Fatima and say "The Rosary will bring peace to the world". For the only peace the world can know is the peace that begins in the heart: "Be still and know that I am God."

# 13 *"All that is mine is yours . . ."*

In the year 1486, Michael de Insulis (François de Lille), O.P., appeared in the University of Cologne at the time of public debates with his *Defence of the Rosary Confraternity*. This was early in the history of printing, yet his treatise was published in several editions all over Europe. Fraternity or fellowship in prayer was very much the thing in those days. With the prayer climate already explained, it can readily be understood that emphasis was on the praying group and their growth in the spirit, rather than on the actual form of the prayer.

## Shared living

The Dominican Rosary was not just a prayer; it was a prayer of a certain way of shared living. The Confraternity member was not one lost in a crowd, but was invited to take a place of honour, to claim his inheritance. And this not for his own sake only, but for the sake of his brother, who might be sick or ignorant or in sin. What men like Michael de Insulis stressed was the *spiritual sharing,* quoting the Vulgate text of Ps. 118:63: "I share all with those who keep your law."

They spoke of sharing the supernatural values not only of our prayers but of our good works. This sharing was to be so generous that they said we should not cling to our own store, but should be willing to share with others. We should make an act of complete consecration to Mary, giving into her care the satisfactory and petition value of our works, so that she might share them with her whole family.

## "All that is mine . . ."

The title of this chapter is borrowed from William Pepin, a contemporary of Michael de Insulis. Pepin preached all over France. In his work, *Salutate Mariam, (Salute Mary)* he highlights the text of Luke 15:31. He recalls the words of the Prodigal's father to the elder brother: "All that I have is yours . . ."

The father gives the elder son a powerful lesson in the importance of sharing. "This prodigal is your brother. We must stand by him, rejoice with him. I have been waiting and praying for him all this time. Now we must rejoice with him and celebrate together."

What's more, the father reminds the elder son: "You didn't have to slave on the farm . . . as a first-born son, all that I have is yours. There was no need to come begging for a kid like a servant. You could have gone and killed the fatted calf yourself. You could have taken out the best cloak and put the ring on your brother's finger yourself."

"So", argues Pepin, "every member of the Brotherhood should leave behind the slave mentality. Being one with Jesus in the mysteries of the Rosary, he shares the blood of the Saviour and becomes a prince of the royal household." As such, he has privileges bringing with them obligations towards his fellows. No need for self pity, or struggling alone. He must learn to live in a way that supports others, and at the same time accept support.

The involvement of the Dominicans with the origins of the Rosary simply as a prayer form is vague and undocumented. Their concern for community or fellowship in prayer, however, stands out like a beacon-light. The name given to this Rosary Society was "The Society of Slaves of Jesus in the chain of the Rosary". But after what Pepin said about the slave-mind of the elder son, it was necessary to point out that there was another slavery: the love-slavery St Paul mentioned, when he admonished his followers to become "slaves of Jesus Christ".

## Grignion De Montfort

Three hundred years later, St Louis Grignion de Montfort, a direct lineal descendant by grace of Alan de la Roche, Michael de Insulis and Pepin, spelt this same message out in another book destined to be buried alive for a further century. The inspiration of the fifteenth century seems to have got lost in legalism and privilege, and we find de Montfort lamenting that there was in his time no "true" confraternity to promote his teaching (cf *Treatise on the True Devotion to the Blessed Virgin*, Chapter 3).

*Fourteenth-century triptych of Simon of Bologna, highlighting the principal elements that have gone to the making of the Rosary. The left-hand panel shows a bishop preaching. On the other side is a nun with a red and white string of beads contemplating the subject of the preaching, which is clearly the mystery of the Son of God born of woman. In the top corners, the Angel is shown making the announcement to Mary. So the "Hail Mary" becomes the thread running through the meditation.*

# 14 *The healing power of the Rosary*

The ministry of healing is coming back in the Church. But what has truly amazed me is that it was all happening in the days of my friend, Pére Bernard of Toulouse. As I turned over the pages of *Le Triple Rosaire* I might as well have been reading the 1977 book, *The Power to Heal,* by my fellow Dominican in the United States, Father Francis McNutt. Indeed, Father Francis himself is the first to admit this, and he encourages Catholics to rediscover their lost heritage.

## The Rosary-lamp oil

On page thirty-six of *Le Triple Rosaire,* one reads:

> In case of illness, members should have recourse with confidence to the oil of the lamp burning before the Rosary Altar – imitating the Confraternity members of Milan who anoint themselves with it and receive great number of cures. They should repeat often the names of Jesus and Mary.

On recounting this discovery to one of my colleagues in Rome, he remarked with a show of pleasant recognition:

> That explains what I often saw the old women do in Tralee. As an altar boy, I observed them go right up to the lamp and boldly pull it down on the chain-pulley. They would dip cotton wool into the oil and bring it home. Clearly, they were doing this under some old instruction – though we never knew whose instruction – and nobody dared ask them, or stop them.

## Formula of blessing

The French instruction, three hundred years earlier, admonishes the director to distribute this oil to his members. From this, as well as from the wording of the "Blessing of Oil" in the Roman ritual, it is clear that the application was done by the laity themselves. The oil would have been blessed either by a Bishop or a priest, and Pére Bernard goes to the trouble of setting down a form of prayer to be used by members of the Rosary Confraternity when they themselves applied the oil to sick members.

*May the Lord Jesus Christ heal you from this illness and (or) anxiety, through the intercession of the Blessed Virgin Mary. In the name of the Father, and the Son, and the Holy Spirit, Amen.*

As well as the physically sick, the oil was applied to those suffering from mental distress, anxiety or scruples. These and other conditions are specifically mentioned.

### Even miracles!

Not only cures by way of gradual healings are spoken of, but miracles too. The prior of the famous Dominican Convent of Milan is referred to as reporting many great miracles. The names and titles of prominent citizens are mentioned. These had been checked by the Cardinal and the whole matter sent for investigation to Rome, where a Book of Records was ordered.

I was glad to read of how Father Francis McNutt, to allay the difficulties of his Protestant friends, pointed out that this kind of practice might be compared to the handkerchiefs touched to St Paul, not deifying Paul but using him as a point of contact with God. It is not Paul, not the oil of the Rosary lamp, that heals. Healing comes from the Lordship of Jesus over all creatures.

### The source of healing

This comes across loud and clear in the case of the Rosary. For the Rosary is a prayer built on the mystery of Jesus, the Jesus who emptied himself, becoming obedient unto death, who has been given a name which is above every name. The more we enter into that Mystery as set forth in Paul's letter to the Philippians, the more the healing power of Christ's salvation becomes available to us.

For my own part, when I apply this oil to the sick, I pray one of the mysteries of the Rosary over the patient, asking him to rest quietly in the name of Jesus. I ask him also to let Mary, who is Mother of the whole Body of Christ, take him into her care.

### St Louis Bertrand

St Louis Bertrand, the Spanish apostle of New Granada, was accustomed to carry a large Rosary round his neck, and one of his favourite practices was to place it about the neck of a sick person.

When he did this to the Countess of Albayda, her illness immediately vanished and her strength was restored. Many miraculous favours were granted to those who reverently used Rosaries blessed by this saint. After his return to Valencia, he gave a Rosary to a friend and told him to preserve it with reverence "because in the Indies this Rosary cured the sick, converted sinners, and, I think, also raised the dead to life".

On another occasion, he spoke more decidedly to a spiritual confidante, saying directly: "God in his mercy granted that this Rosary should raise the dead to life." Thus, his devotion to the Rosary betrayed him into revealing a miracle he had sought to conceal: the raising of a girl to life during his South American mission. The report spread among the natives and reached Valencia, but the Saint would not either acknowledge it or deny its truth. Once, when asked so directly that he could not hedge, he replied: "What makes you ask such a question? God does what a blacksmith would do when making an iron tool: he has many suitable pieces of material and selects the one he pleases, although all are fit for his purpose."

### The healing of brotherhood

Apart from the Lord's choice of a particular individual or tool for his purpose, the Rosary Confraternity brought an added dimension to this ministry of healing: that is, the charity of the members among themselves, the expectant faith and love that bound them together, in the Lord.

The gift of healing is one of the charismatic gifts mentioned by St Paul in his letter to the Corinthians. Now Paul is insistent that the source of these gifts is the love which is poured out by the Holy Spirit. Nothing hinders Divine healing so much as division among the brethren, and nothing lets it flow so abundantly as the bond of love and the fellowship of the Holy Spirit. Fraternity is a vital element in the healing ministry. The members take to heart the words of Jesus: "Where two or three are gathered together in my name, there am I in the midst of them."

*This is a type of triptych found widely in fourteenth-century art and helpful for getting to the origins of the Dominican approach to the Rosary. The central theme is the Mother and Child scheme of salvation.*

*In the side panels there are details corresponding roughly with our fifteen mysteries, though not exactly, as these had not clearly emerged at that time. One mystery portrayed is "The Manifestation or Epiphany of Jesus, in his Baptism". It is significant that in several modern schemes for Rosary mysteries this one is frequently mentioned.*

*The top corners have the Angel Gabriel on one side and Mary on the other, this being the nucleus of the other mysteries.*

# 15 *The ecumenical links of the Rosary*

I believe I have given more presents of Rosary-beads to Protestant friends than to Catholics. So let me repeat the offer which has appeared on Rosary Apostolate literature over the years: "If you are a Catholic, give a Rosary to your other Christian friends. If you are not, and are too shy to approach a Roman Catholic, drop a note to me or to the Rosary Apostolate, and we will see that you get a gift of a Rosary beads!"

Mary and other Churches

In *Marialis Cultus* (by the way, the translation of that document can be quite misleading if rendered "Marian Cult". It is better translated into English as "Devotion to Mary"), Pope Paul VI calls attention to the glorious tradition of Marian piety in the Orthodox Churches. He goes on to say that "Catholics are united with Anglicans, whose classical theologians have already drawn attention to the sound Scriptural basis for devotion to the Mother of our Lord, while Anglicans of the present day increasingly underline the importance of Mary's place in the Christian life" (par. 32).

The Holy Father points out, too, that the Church desires that "any manifestation of piety which is opposed to correct practice should be eliminated, and every care must be exercised to avoid exaggerations which could mislead other Christian brethren".

True devotion to Mary must be "an approach to Christ, the source and centre of ecclesiastical communion, in which all who confess that Jesus is God and Lord, Saviour and sole Mediator *(1 Tim 2:5),* are called to be one; with one another, with Christ, and with the Father in the unity of the Holy Spirit" (par. 32).

As far back as 1948, Wilfred Jukka, a de Montfort father, was writing:

> "You can't shock a New Yorker." That used to be a boast of the people of that city. Perhaps it still is. Yet I rather imagine that even they got something of a shock when they read one morning that a leading Methodist in the U.S.A. had been urging Protestants to say the Rosary.
>
> It happened when Dr. James A. Beebe told the students at Allegheny

College that Protestant prayer had suffered because it lacked a system of controlled meditation. He said that the Catholic Rosary, with its definite symbols, held the mind, and he urged other churches to utilise this method of prayer.

This speech of Dr. Beebe's was reported in *The Times* (April 25, 1948) and it caused quite a sensation. He had been Dean of the School of Theology at Boston University until he became President of Allegheny. So he was quite important in Protestant circles.

His words gave rise to much dark foreboding about "another one going Roman." However, as far as we know, he remained a staunch Methodist – and he continued to advise his co-religionists to use the Rosary.

He is not the only Protestant to seize upon the possibilities of the Rosary as a way of uniting souls to Christ.

The whole idea of the Rosary is that it gives us a short, *definite* time to reflect on some *definite* event in the life of Christ. It is a sort of long-term policy which is guaranteed, if used frequently, to lead souls ever nearer to Jesus.

## Lutheran testimony

The testimony of Richard Baumann, a minister of the Evangelical Lutheran Church of Württemberg, is striking:

When the rosary is said, truth sinks into the subconscious like a slow and steady downpour, the hammered sentences of the cathechism receive an indelible validity for precisely the little ones, the least, to whom belongs the kingdom of heaven (Matt. 19.49).

It is a long and persevering gaze, a meditation, a quieting of the spirit in the praise of God, the value of which we Protestants are learning once more. In this chain of love, the cross is the dominant symbol, the beads being a prop for the memory, a help against impatience, so that a set length of time may be adhered to. The whole is, therefore, an aid to prayer , of which history has known many – a sign of the condescension of God our Saviour.

But now to the invoking of Mary! "Hail Mary, full of grace, The Lord is with thee. Blessed are thou among women, and blessed is the Fruit of thy womb, Jesus." This is biblical! It is the greeting of the angel and of Elizabeth found in the first chapter of the Gospel according to St Luke. Christians join in his salutation and the biblical prophecy comes true: "Behold from henceforth all generations shall call be blessed, for he that is mighty hath done great things; and holy is his name" *(Luke 1, 48-9)*. All generations – that is to the end of the world.

Mary is not thought of by them as dead but as living wholly with the Lord. "We believe that long ago she reached the first resurrection", said Friedrich Christoph Otinger. There is fellowship with her – that she is greeted in the words if scripture is proof of it. She is seen very close to Jesus, as once it was and as was promised at the beginning of the history of salvation *(Gen. 3, 15):* now she is present, in a heavenly way, for God's people too, and truly close to them.

## Anglican viewpoint

The Reverend Gerard Irvine, an Anglican clergyman attached to the Parish of St Matthew, Westminster, London, gives the following testimony:

I am a cradle member of the Church of England, the corresponding number across the Celtic Sea of the Church of Ireland. And all my life I have used the Rosary.

Although I would not naturally describe myself as a Protestant – indeed every day of my life I say in the Creed that "I believe in the Holy Catholic Church" – in my childhood I certainly did not come under Roman Catholic influence. On my father's side I am of Ulster Protestant stock; I spent most of my childhood in a west country village whose Catholics had to go a good many miles to get to Mass. There was not any particular feeling against Catholics; they just didn't enter the local picture.

### My first Roman Catholic

I well remember the first time I very consciously set eyes on a Roman Catholic. I was aged about eight, and was staying with a godmother at the seaside. I was told that the guest coming to lunch was a Roman Catholic. I kept my eyes glued on this perfectly nice ordinary woman, hoping to find some eccentricity of behaviour or appearance, and was, of course, disappointed. In my childhood I never met a Roman Catholic priest or religious, and do not remember ever being taken to a Roman Catholic church.

I was taken every Sunday to the local parish church – and I must explain that that means that I was taken every Sunday to the Anglican Eucharist. During the service I was given a Rosary by my mother. I was told to think of as many terms of endearment for Jesus as I could, while I passed my fingers over the beads; and then think of all the people I ought to pray for. So I grew up with the idea of a Rosary as an accompaniment to prayer.

### Taught to love Our Lady

At the same time I was taught to love and trust Our Lady, and to ask her prayers. This, too, was a normal part of my devotional life. But I do not think that at first I associated the Rosary with devotion to the Virgin. Perhaps I should have done so, as I had a Rosary with a view of Lourdes in the middle of the Cross, and I knew the story of Bernadette. But, in fact, it was not until my early 'teens that I put the use of the Rosary and the Hail Mary together. I discovered, in an Anglican book of devotion called "The Century Prayer Book", instructions on the fifteen Mysteries. I immediately set myself to use the Rosary in the traditional Catholic way.

Difficult at first

At first, I remember, I found it extremely difficult. I now see I tried too hard to do too many things at once: to 'mean' with maximum concentration every word of the prayers, AND picture the scene, AND think about it. I soon learned to try less hard, and found it correspondingly more profitable. Since then I have never been without a Rosary, and have said it regularly.

At my theological college it was the custom (though not in any sense a rule) for the students to recite the Rosary in front of the Blessed Sacrament before lunch each day. I got into the habit of doing this, and began to make the Mysteries, said 'with intention' my normal method of intercession, thus reverting to the habits of childhood.

At College in Oxford I was a pupil of that great saint and scholar, Austin Farrer, then Chaplain of Trinity. He devotes a chapter of one of his books to the Rosary, which he calls "the heaven-sent aid". The lapidary reflections on the Mysteries in that chapter have helped me more than anything else I have ever read, and still are the background of my praying. I sometimes still make use of his suggestion that during the Sorrowful Mysteries one can substitute for the ten Hail Marys the prayer "O Saviour of the world, who by thy Cross and precious blood, hast redeemed us, save us and help us, we humbly beseech thee, O Lord".

Other use of the beads

In recent years I have come to value the Eastern Orthodox use of the Rosary as an accompaniment to the hundred repetitions of the "Jesus Prayer" – "Lord Jesus Christ, Son of the Living God, have mercy on me a sinner". It is interesting to discover that once again I am returning to the method of using the Rosary that my mother taught me all those years ago.

When the time comes . . .

The set of beads I have been using for the last fifteen years are very precious to me. They were made from pressed leaves by the Religious of the Cartuja de Miraflores in Spain, and still retain the ghost of a perfume of roses. But what makes them particularly valued is that they were individually blessed for me by Pope John XXIII. I hope that when the time comes they may accompany me into the coffin. But much more, I hope that the Mother whose prayers I invoke when I say the Rosary, will then show me "the blessed fruit of Her womb, Jesus".

## Methodist tribute

After such spontaneous ecumenical testimonies, there is not much point in further comment. But may I pay tribute to that fine Methodist, J. Neville Ward, who has given us one of the best books on the Rosary in recent times, with the intriguing title: *Five for Sorrow, Ten for Joy.* In his Preface he writes:

> If anyone were to ask why a Methodist comes to be using a Rosary, I would give two reasons. There has to be change and variety in the means one uses for maintaining Christian outlook and aspiration, or else the life of faith becomes dull. An obvious way of doing this, in these days of increasing ecumenical encounter and exchange, is to attempt to pray with helps not used in one's own tradition but widely employed elsewhere in the life of the Church. There is a double advantage, the stimulus of praying in a new way, and the widening of one's experience of the fellowship of the Spirit.
>
> The second and clearly related reason is that in Methodism the silence about the Mother of Jesus is positively deafening. It is so complete that during a ministry of over thirty years I have begun to wonder what anxiety is behind this surprising mental hang-up. This wonder has increased as I have learned how much she means in the public and private praying of both the Roman Catholic and the Orthodox Churches and, incidentally but importantly, as I begin to discover among our own people signs of shy but nervous interest in her mysterious being.

# *Appendix*

Suggestions for a Rosary Service

These suggestions derive from the Apostolic Exhortation *(Marialis Cultus)* of Pope Paul VI, February 1974. In paragraph 51, the Holy Father shows his awareness of new forms of prayer that commend themselves to the rising generation. And he recommends the insertion into the Rosary of scripture readings and a homily. Song, too, he says, will enhance the Rosary. And instead of rushing through this prayer, he suggests having silent pauses. That's easy to remember. In English it might be called the "4S" formula: *Scripture, Sermon, Song, Silence.*

Add another "S" if you like for *saying* the decade, the idea being to intersperse the decades with the above items. However, it might be better to avoid the expression "saying" the decade and think instead in terms of "celebrating" just one mystery at a particular session. Some have found it better to set aside a given time for celebrating the Rosary in this way, rather than specifying a fixed number of decades.

"Jesus clauses"

Paragraph 46 of *Marialis Cultus* treats of the custom of "adding to the name of Jesus in each Hail Mary a reference to the mystery being contemplated". "This was done", adds Pope Paul, "to help contemplation and to make the mind and the voice act in unison". Suggestions for "Jesus clauses" are to be found in the appropriate chapter of this book. Feel free to compose your own. You may find, too, that saying the actual clause disturbs your contemplation. If so, to recall it at the beginning of the mystery, or to silently advert to it in each Ave, may be more satisfactory.

Prayer for the grace of each mystery

*O Mary, Mother of the Church,*
*Teach me to accept God's will in the spirit of the Annunciation.*
*Visit us in our need as you visited Elizabeth.*
*Bring us forth in grace, as you brought forth Jesus in the flesh.*
*Present us in the temple of the Father.*
*And take us, after this life's journey, to find Jesus in his Father's House.*

*Obtain for us the courage to be one with Jesus in his agony and to say "Father, your will be done";*
*Grant that "through his wounds" we may be healed;*
*Teach us the meekness of our King crowned with thorns, and how to carry our cross daily,*
*That we may "know the fellowship of his sufferings" on Mount Calvary.*
*And when the hour comes to leave this world, grant that we may "know the power of his resurrection"; and ascend to that home prepared for us.*
*O Mary, sweet Spouse of the Spirit, grant that we may share in the out-pouring of the Holy Spirit;*
*And after this our exile, rejoice in the glory of your assumption*
*And coronation in heaven. Amen.*

## Prayer themes for each of the fifteen mysteries

### Joyful Mysteries

*The annunciation to Mary*
O God, I pray in this mystery that I may be a door, through which your living Word may enter. Give me a mind open to your light, give me a heart ever open to your love, give me hands open to your service. So may I place myself in your hands that in and through me, you may enter your own World as once you entered it through the open door of Mary.

*The visitation of Mary to Elizabeth*
The very sound of your voice filled Elizabeth with the Holy Spirit, so that the child in her womb leapt for joy; and she herself cried aloud: "Blessed are you among women, and blessed is the fruit of your womb." Let your voice, Mary, sound now in my ears, so that I, too, being filled with the Holy Spirit, may call you blessed and experience within me the joy that comes from the Christ-child you bring to every man.

*The birth of Jesus*
O Jesus, I accept you right now as my personal Saviour, Christ the Lord. Father, I thank you for so precious a gift. With the angels in heaven I praise you for Jesus. "Glory to God in highest heaven, and on earth his peace for men on whom his favour rests."

*Jesus is presented in the Temple*
O Mary and Joseph, come to the temple of my heart; come to me with your Divine Child. He is the light to all who sit in darkness and in the shadow of death. He is the true light, enlightening every man coming into the world. May I go to meet Christ in every man who presents himself at the door of my heart.

*The finding of Jesus in the Temple*
Take me by the hand now, dearest Mother, and lead me into the dark corners of my own soul. Show me there Jesus, my Master. Let me experience the power of his words, and the light of his wisdom. Teach me, too, to find him in the temple of my neighbour's heart; so that in every one that I meet, I may find Jesus.

## Sorrowful Mysteries

*The agony in the Garden*
Dear Jesus, Gethsemene has grown great, the cup of life's sorrows is the same that would not pass you by. Grant us, in this mystery, to say: "Father, your will be done . . ." Give us generosity to share the bitter cup of life's sorrows pressed to the lips of our brothers, so that we may not refuse to be part of the agony of our times.

*The scourging of Jesus*
Sweet Jesus, by your bruises we are healed. Your passion is like a great healing medicine where sins are taken away and health restored. By this mystery of your scourging, I call upon you to save me.

*Jesus is crowned with thorns*
Lord, your head was crowned for my sins of vanity and pride, and for all the impure and unjust thoughts that flood my soul. By this saving mystery I ask that you would give me a new heart. Lord, by your overpowering humility make us patient, and give us the light to see you as King, claiming sweet dominion over our minds and hearts.

*Jesus carries his Cross*
"Unless a man takes up a cross each day and follows me," you said, "he cannot be my disciple." I can't just sit and contemplate the cross, I must accept it. I pray for the vision to see Christ my Lord ahead of me, as he leads the way: "Do not be afraid, I have covered every step of the way before you, and I am with you now. Just follow me."

*The Crucifixion*
Lord, you are more than ever the Master of Prayer in this hour. In union with you, I beg forgiveness of the Eternal Father. Father, forgive us. We know what we do. With the good thief, I cry: "Jesus, remember me when you come into your kingly power." Let me hear that consoling reply: "Truly, I say to you, today you will be with me in Paradise."

## Glorious Mysteries

*The Resurrection*

Lord, we believe that if we share your sufferings, we will come to know the power of your resurrection. "We are already citizens of heaven and from heaven we expect our deliverer to come, the Lord Jesus Christ. He will transfigure the body belonging to our humble state and give it a form like that of his own resplendent body *(Philippians 3).*

O Risen Christ, be Lord of my life. Take me and transform me. Let my body and all its powers yield to the glory that comes from your glorified body, so that my weakness may be turned into strength.

*The Ascension*

"We pray that the God of Our Lord Jesus Christ, the all-glorious Father, may give us the spiritual powers of wisdom and vision, by which there comes the knowledge of him. We pray that our inward eyes may be illuminated, so that we may know what is the hope to which he calls us, what the wealth and the glory of the share he offers us among his people in their heritage, and how vast the resources of his power open to us who trust in him" *(Ephesians 1).*

*The descent of the Holy Spirit*

Spirit of the living God, you moved over the darkness and there was light. You came like a breath of wind over the dead waters and brought them to life. Come, Holy Spirit, in this mystery that we may be baptised in new waters. Let fountains of living water spring up within us. Let rivers of life flow out from us into the desert.

Father, fill us with the power of your Holy Spirit, that we may be witnesses to your name. Open our eyes to things unseen.

*The assumption of Our Lady into Heaven*

Dear Mother, you have gone home, lifted up on high by the wounded hands of your Son. Grant that these hands be stretched down from heaven to lift us, too, from this vale of tears.

O Jesus, we cry to your mother and ours "that she who aided the beginnings of the Church by her prayers, may now intercede before her Son in the fellowship of all the saints, until all be gathered into one people of God".

*Our Lady is crowned Queen of Heaven*

"And a great sign appeared in heaven, a woman clothed with the sun, with the moon under her feet, and on her head a crown of twelve stars."

O Mary, the loving service that you gave at Nazareth in the house of Elizabeth, at Cana and Golgotha, has not ended. As Queen of heaven and earth, as mother of the Church, you are one with the Church's maternal concern that all men should come to knowledge of the truth, and share in the salvation which was merited for them by Christ's death.

For a prayer group situation

Any part of scripture can be material for sharing, as all scripture points in the long run to the Lordship of Jesus. So with the Bible in one hand and the beads in the other, people are getting together to pray in a free spontaneous way, interspersing the Paters and Aves with praise and petition and readings from the Old and New Testaments.

The keynote of this type of meeting is openness to the Holy Spirit, and not structuring things unduly. The leader should be sensitive to the promptings of the Lord and the leading of the Spirit, but should not dominate the meeting.

There should be time for listening and for silence. In such situations one should be open to the prophetic word of God. There should also be a great openness to each other. When people start sharing their prayer, they begin to share their lives. They commit their lives to the Lord and to each other. This is the basis of the Rosary Confraternity. Indeed, without some commitment or covenant of this kind, fraternity in the full Christian sense is missing. Perhaps it is at this deeper level that we must search for renewal in the Rosary.

# Notes on sources

As this is a book about "rediscovering", most help came from pottering around old libraries. Such a wealth of material still exists, ranging over five hundred years, that it is not possible to catalogue everything. For this reason I content myself with giving general remarks that might help a future explorer.

For the reader of Italian, the best place to begin is Rome. The Vatican and Cassanatense Libraries have between them hundreds of old volumes classified under "Rosario della Gloriosa Vergine," and "Psalterium Mariae". Many of these contain exciting illustrations, at least for those early days of printing. While most of the material is in Italian, there is quite and amount also in Latin.

The book constantly quoted in this present work, *Le Triple Rosaire* by Pére Bernard of Toulouse, is in the Library of the Irish Dominicans, at San Clemente. It contains such a huge amount of sheer print and illustration as to be off-putting at first sight. But in all my twenty-five years of searching I never came across anything like it as a mine of Rosary information. The copy in San Clemente is the third edition of 1676.

There is a welcome for any serious student of the Rosary at Sancta Maria Novella in Florence, with its wonderful collection of old Dominican books, and there is a chance to pick up reprints of some old masters. *Salutate Mariam,* by the seventeenth century William Pepinus, O.P., is especially helpful for understanding the true nature of the Rosary Confraternity. It was in this ancient Dominican house that I met Fr Stefano Orlandi, O.P., noted historian and zealous promotor of the Perpetual Rosary, and was told of the Rosary significance of the *Arnolfini Wedding* painting. In 1965, Fr Orlandi brought out his comprehensive study *Libro del Rosario della Gloriosa Vergine Maria.* The bibliography with this work is very useful.

The National Library, Paris, has five copies of the very earliest printed work on the Rosary Confraternity. These volumes were so beautifully produced and so priceless even in the time of Napoleon, that he had them brought as war booty from Italy. As mentioned in my own text, the author, Michael de Insulis (François de Lille) prepared this defence of the Fraternity for the time of public debate in the University of Cologne.

One thing which must not go unmentioned is the *Index of Art,* now housed in the Vatican Library, Rome. The index is of American origin. Don't be surprised at finding Rosary classified under "Utensil". Under this general heading, subheaded "Rosary", you can track down many examples of art, painting, mosaic, sculpture, where a string of prayer beads occurs. This guide led me to art galleries where, in the thirteenth- and fourteenth-century sections, I could see things not recorded in print.

Nearer to Ireland, and to our own times, there is *Hasting's Dictionary of Religion and Ethics,* which supplied most of the material for the chapter on the evolution of the Rosary. *The Rose-Garden Game* by Eithne Wilkins of the University of Reading is a scholarly book telling the story of "rosaries" from round the world.

On the Irish traditional scene, Fr Conleth Kearns, O.P., of San Clemente, has a private study of Irish manuscripts on the "Saltair Mhuire". The Irish Folklore Commission has an interesting collection of items including photographs of beautiful old Irish rosaries.

*The Catholic Encyclopaedia* of the first years of this century has all the controversial material of the late Fr Thurston, S.J.. It makes an interesting contrast to study the Rosary article in the New American version. From America also, comes the translation into English of Franz Michael Willam's *The Rosary* (Benziger). This is a clear and simple analysis of the development of the Catholic Rosary tradition. The United States provides as well, a reprint of St Louis Grignon's classic, *The Secret of the Rosary.*

On the official level, there is *Marialis Cultus* of Pope Paul VI. The duplicated *Notes of the International Rosary Congress* (Rome, May 1976) gives a survey of Rosary thought and action throughout the world, showing the growing plurality of practice now prevailing. With statements from the Master General of the Dominican Order and from Dominican national directors from every continent, these notes are a must for any serious student.

# Notes on Cover illustrations

*Front Cover*

*The Great Rosary Window,*
*Black Abbey, Kilkenny, Ireland*

*This is the largest and most magnificent window of its kind in Ireland. It is regarded as the major work done in the country during the second half of the fourteenth century. The glass was renewed during the nineteenth century. Writing from the newly restored Black Abbey, Kilkenny, the author says:*

> *You have only to sit in silence before this vast and glorious panorama of scripture to realise that the Rosary is simply a way of letting in the Gospel light through fifteen windows of the spirit.*
>
> *The arrangement of the mysteries, with the Crucifixion in the middle and the Ascension placed halfway through the Glorious mysteries, is a unique feature of the window. This gives rise to a central axis down the middle: birth, death and exaltation, around which the other mysteries revolve.*
>
> *Visitors are at first disturbed by this departure from the traditional time sequence of the mysteries. But they are agreeably surprised to find that in the most recent Papal study of the Rosary,* Marialis Cultus, *Pope Paul VI distinguished between the "chronological order of the facts" and the "original proclamation of the faith which the Rosary reflects". The core text of the Rosary, according to the Pope, is that of St Paul to the Philippians, where he writes of Jesus taking on the nature of a slave (Nativity), obedient unto death (Crucifixion) and exalted as Lord (Ascension).*
>
> *Since Pope Paul set it down on paper, much of that instruction has failed to find a mouth to proclaim it or an ear to hear it. I know of no place where the message is more clearly portrayed and readily grasped than in the great Rosary window of the Black Abbey. With the morning sunlight streaming through it, the window stands in all its glory, a challenge to renewal and a call to a rediscovery of the full potential of the Rosary.*

*Back Cover*

*An alabaster representation of the Trinity from the Black Abbey, Kilkenny, officially The Church of the Most Holy Trinity. The statue has 1264 on its base, but it thought to have been carved at Bristol about 1400. It recalls the original Christological and Trinitarian thrust of the Rosary as presented by the first Dominican preachers who saw it more as a "method of preaching than of praying".*

*Pope Paul VI reminds us that "exercises of piety directed to the Virgin Mary should clearly express the Trinitarian and Christological note that is intrinsic and essential to them"* (Marialis Cultus, *Par. 25*). *It is interesting, too, to remember that the first lesson that Our Lady taught St Bernadette in the Grotto of Lourdes was to make the Sign of the Cross in the name of the Father, and of the Son and of the Holy Spirit.*

# About the Author

Tom Harty joined the Dominican Order in 1949, taking the name Gabriel, having been a priest in the Archdiocese of Dublin for four years. He was chosen by the Master General himself to be a promoter of the Rosary in Ireland. For years he studied the Dominican traditions from Latin, Italian and French sources, and he dreams of a Rosary revival taking its inspiration from the original charism of the Order.

In the early days, Fr Gabriel campaigned in the North of Ireland with the Bible in one hand and the beads in the other, often being warned: "They'll take you for a Protestant!" Inspired by the passage in the Gospel of the ancient Dominican Mass of the Rosary, "Jesus went around from one city and village to another proclaiming the Kingdom" *(Luke 8: 1-10),* he regarded his apostolate as a form of itinerant preaching. He spearheaded the industrial Rosary movement of the 1950s and 1960s in factories and workshops all over the country, often sleeping on the side of the road.

Now, after a quarter of a century as National Director of the Rosary, Fr Gabriel is still challenged by Luke's words: "The twelve were with him, and also some women." He believes they are a call to a rediscovering of a more evangelical style of travelling Rosary-mission.